5

Alpacas have soft hair called fleece or fibre. Alpaca fleece can be 22 different colours, including white, brown, black and silver.

Pebble® Plus

FARM ANIMALS

ALPACAS

by Michelle Hasselius

Consultant: Anna Firshman, BVSc, PhD, DACVIM
Department of Veterinary Population Medicine
University of Minnesota, USA

raintree

a Capstone company — publishers for children

Raintree is an imprint of Capstone Global Library Limited, a company incorporated in England and Wales having its registered office at 264 Banbury Road, Oxford, OX2 7DY – Registered company number: 6695582

www.raintree.co.uk
myorders@raintree.co.uk

Printed and bound in China.

Editorial Credits
Michelle Hasselius, editor; Kayla Rossow, designer; Pam Mitsakos, media researcher;
Katy LaVigne, production specialist

ISBN 978 1 4747 2240 7 (hardback)
20 19 18 17 16
10 9 8 7 6 5 4 3 2 1

ISBN 978 1 4747 2264 3 (paperback)
21 20 19 18 17
10 9 8 7 6 5 4 3 2 1

British Library Cataloguing in Publication Data
A full catalogue record for this book is available from the British Library.

Acknowledgements
Shutterstock: Aneta_Gu, 10–11, bluedogroom, 5, Dieter Hawlan, 6–7, Eky Studio, (back cover background), Elenamiv, 22 (background), hjochen, 15, Karyl Miller, 13, Kookkai_nak, 1 (background), meunierd, 16–17, Milosz_G, cover, 1, ostill, 19; Thinkstock: astonerattnet, 9, suefeldberg, 20–21

The author would like to thank Dr Anna Firshman for her invaluable help in the preparation of this book.

Every effort has been made to contact copyright holders of material reproduced in this book. Any omissions will be rectified in subsequent printings if notice is given to the publisher.

All the internet addresses (URLs) given in this book were valid at the time of going to press. However, due to the dynamic nature of the internet, some addresses may have changed, or sites may have changed or ceased to exist since publication. While the author and publisher regret any inconvenience this may cause readers, no responsibility for any such changes can be accepted by either the author or the publisher.

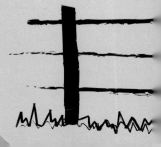

Farmers can own two different kinds of alpaca. Huacayas have short, wavy fleece. They look like teddy bears. Suri alpacas have silky, wavy fleece.

Huacaya (wuh-KAY-uh)
Suri (SUR-ee)

Suri alpacas

Alpacas are related to camels and llamas. But alpacas are smaller. They weigh up to 84 kilograms (185 pounds). Alpacas live for about 20 years.

Adults and babies

Alpacas grow up on the farm. Baby alpacas are called crias. Crias weigh about 7.7 kilograms (17 pounds) at birth. Female alpacas are called hembras. Males are called machos.

cria (KREE-uh)
hembra (em-BRAH)
macho (mah-CHOH)

crias

An alpaca eats grass and hay.
The chewed food travels into
one of the alpaca's three stomach
chambers. Later the alpaca burps
up the food and chews it again.

On the farm

Alpacas stay together in a herd. They communicate by humming. Alpacas also make loud, high calls when scared or angry.

Farmers keep alpacas for their fleece. Alpaca fleece is soft and warm. Farmers shear the fleece each spring. Fleece can be made into clothing or blankets.

fleece

Foxes and other predators attack alpacas. Farmers use donkeys or dogs to keep predators away. Alpacas also need sheds. Alpacas stay safe on the farm.

Glossary

camel   animal with a round hump on its back

chamber   enclosed space in an animal's body

communicate   share information, thoughts or feelings

fleece   coat of soft, fluffy hair that covers animals such as alpacas, sheep and llamas; fleece is also called fibre

herd   large group of animals that lives or moves together

hum   make a steady, buzzing noise

nibble   bite something gently

predator   animal that hunts other animals for food

shear   cut off or trim; a farmer shears an alpaca's fleece so it can be used to make cloth

shed   small building

Read more

Farm Animals (Tadpole Learners), Annabelle Lynch (Franklin Watts, 2015)

Farm Animals: True or False? (True or False?), Daniel Nunn (Raintree, 2013)

Llamas (South American Animals), Mary R. Dunn (Capstone Press, 2012)

Websites

www.cbc.ca/kidscbc2/the-feed/fun-facts-about-cute-animals-alpaca-edition
Learn interesting facts about alpacas.

www.omdfarm.co.uk/essex_east_london/fun_farm_animal_facts/alpacas/index.htm
Read about alpaca statistics, learn fun facts and play games.

Index